I Fall
to
My Knees

I Fall to My Knees

DEVOTIONAL PRAYERS INSPIRED BY EPHESIANS 3

LAURA FREUDIG

BARBOUR BOOKS

An Imprint of Barbour Publishing, Inc.

© 2013 by Barbour Publishing, Inc.

ISBN 978-1-68322-755-7

Published by Barbour Books, an imprint of Barbour Publishing, Inc., 1810 Barbour Drive, Uhrichsville, Ohio 44683, www.barbourbooks.com

Our mission is to inspire the world with the life-changing message of the Bible.

 Member of the
Evangelical Christian
Publishers Association

Printed in the United States of America.

Contents

Introduction

At the height of its power, Ephesus was second only to Rome. The city had a population of 500,000, sophisticated public baths and aqueducts, and a 25,000-seat theater for plays and gladiatorial contests. It boasted a bustling harbor and the great Temple of Artemis, one of the seven wonders of the ancient world.

But only a few centuries later, all had changed. The city had been sacked by the Goths and the temple destroyed. Most significantly, the harbor, lifeblood of travel and trade in the ancient world, slowly filled with silt. Today, the ruins of Ephesus sit miles from the sea.

Just as the buildup of silt spelled death to an ancient city, our hearts can become silted without a constant flow of Living Water. In this book, you will find prayers and devotions based on Paul's prayer in Ephesians 3:14–21, which will inspire you to drink deeply the living water that only Jesus Christ can offer.

I Fall to My
Knees and Pray

*She had the apron flung over her head, while an endless
flow of children eddied and swirled around her knees
and in and out of the room. They knew not to bother her,
because when her apron was over her head,
Susanna Wesley was praying.*

*Most of us won't have nineteen children, or raise them
without electricity, running water, refrigerators, or indoor
toilets. But the distractions that keep us from prayer are
just as real. Have you ever kneeled to pray, then started
to itch? Remembered you had to do something. . .else?
The devil doesn't want us to pray, and he'll use whatever
it takes to stop us. It doesn't have to be nineteen children
if an itch on the elbow will do. Susanna's perseverance
produced the great Christian soldiers John and
Charles Wesley, a preacher and a hymn writer.
The battle begins on our knees.*

Come Closer, Beloved

Dear Lord, You are the God of the universe, and yet You ask me to come closer. I can't stand in Your presence, yet You ask me to approach with freedom and confidence. It's all because of Jesus, Lord, that I can do this! I praise You for the great gift of Your Son, who allows me this access to You, my creator. I am so small, but I long to know You better. I am so weak, but I know You have power to spare. Help me to come to You again and again. In Jesus' precious name, amen.

In him and through faith in him we may approach God with freedom and confidence.

Ephesians 3:12 NIV

In Your Presence This Day

Dear Father, I thank You that Your ear is always listening for the cries of Your people. You are always listening for my voice, and You know it out of billions of others. My words are not just spoken to the empty air, but You give them Your attention. Forgive me for my sins today, Lord, for they are many. I rest under Your mercy.

"If my people, who are called by my name, will humble themselves and pray and seek my face and turn from their wicked ways, then I will hear from heaven."

2 CHRONICLES 7:14 NIV

Do It Anyway

◆━━━━━━━━◆

Oh Lord, I am so tired right now. My eyes ache, my head feels tight, and all I want to do is crawl back into bed. Already the demands of the day are pressing at me, calling me to leave You before I've even really started talking with You. Upstairs the baby is calling from his crib, "Dada! Mama!" And that's what I feel like. Father! Lord! I want You. I need You. Please come to me right here, in these short minutes, and magnify them into peace and grace for the rest of this day. Amen.

But to You I cry, O Lord; and in the morning
shall my prayer come to meet You.

PSALM 88:13 AMPC

Arise and Go

So many times, Lord, I feel the urge to drop to my knees and pray. Yet I don't. Embarrassment, busyness, a dirty floor—they can all stop me from heeding Your call. Yet I praise You that You keep calling my name again and again. Please help me to trust You enough to stop what I am doing when I hear Your call. I am on my knees now, my King. I am listening to Your voice.

The word which came to Jeremiah from the LORD, saying: "Arise and go down to the potter's house, and there I will cause you to hear My words."

JEREMIAH 18:1–2 NKJV

In the Inner Room

Dear God, You know how often I pray and how I often *don't*. You know that sometimes I use it as a weapon. "Lord, give me patience!" I say in the presence of those who are vexing me. Please forgive me. That is not prayer. And Lord, forgive me for *not* praying. Forgive me for wasting the quiet moments that You give me with things that will be forgotten in eternity. I want to know You now, *here*, even before I am with You forever. Amen.

"But you, when you pray, go into your inner room, close your door and pray to your Father who is in secret, and your Father who sees what is done in secret will reward you."

MATTHEW 6:6 NASB

I Will Hear

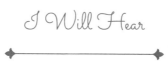

Dear Lord, I praise You that You are the God who hears. I praise You that You know my heart even before *I* do. I rest in the fact that You are answering my prayer, even before I pray. Help me to be more like You, Lord. So often I don't take the time to listen with love to the people around me. And while they are still speaking, I say no. I need Your ears and Your heart, Lord. Speak to me and through me. Amen.

> *"Before they call I will answer;*
> *while they are still speaking I will hear."*

ISAIAH 65:24 NIV

His Will

Dear Lord, there are so many things I want. Sometimes I feel like my prayers are just a long list of wishes, as though You're some sort of celestial genie. But I'm so thankful You are not. You don't give me what I want, just because I want it. I thank You that You give me only what is in line with Your will for me. So, Lord, show me what that is. Reveal Your will, and show me how and for what You want me to pray.

Now this is the confidence that we have in Him, that if we ask anything according to His will, He hears us.

1 John 5:14 nkjv

Good Gifts

——◆——

Lord, You are good. You are good! You are a loving, generous God, slow to anger and rich in love. I pray that the riches You offer through Christ Jesus would be visible in my life, so that others would be drawn to You. I have nothing to offer them except You, Jesus. But You have so much, and You long to open the storehouses of heaven to us, blessings pressed down and running over. Amen.

"If you then, being evil, know how to give good gifts to your children, how much more will your Father who is in heaven give what is good to those who ask Him!"

MATTHEW 7:11 NASB

Alchemy for a Rainy Day

—◆—

Dear Lord, it's so dark this morning. I know You've already pushed the sun up over the horizon: it is day, though it doesn't feel like it. I don't want to have to pray this morning, Lord. I just want to be where You are. I don't want to be here, in this gray light, with a longer grayness stretching before me, then darkness again. I want to be with You, walking on streets of gold, with the light of Your glory shining on my face. I long for that endless golden day, Lord. But I am here, and You are not far off. Please come to me, Lord, and shine Your love and light on my heart this morning. Amen.

My voice shalt thou hear in the morning, O LORD;
in the morning will I direct my prayer
unto thee, and will look up.

PSALM 5:3 KJV

Falling

Dear Father, we started falling in Eden, and we haven't hit bottom yet. Today I said some things I regret. And the things I didn't say (the things only *You* heard) were even worse. I hurt people I care about, and worse, I hurt You, Lord. I am so sorry. Please forgive me. Please redeem my angry, selfish words. I am so glad that You tell us in Your Word to forgive seventy times seven times because I know that is how many times You will forgive me. Thanks be to Jesus, when I fall, I am falling into Your arms. Amen.

Cast your cares on the LORD and he will sustain you;
he will never let the righteous be shaken.

PSALM 55:22 NIV

The Missing P

Dear Father, today I just want to praise You! I spend so much time repenting (read *sinning*), asking (complaining), and yielding (pretending not to be so stubborn), and so little telling You how much I love You. You are merciful, You are awesome, You are holy! You are beyond compare. You are my maker and sustainer. You saved me! You are light and love and all that is good. Lord, You made *mountains*. And trees that spear the clouds, and birds as bright as rainbows, and flowers as small and perfect as a baby's fingernail. Who is like You? Amen and amen and amen.

> *"For then you will delight in the Almighty*
> *and lift up your face to God."*

JOB 22:26 NASB

Expecting Miracles

Dear God, I come before You today, knowing You are a God who works miracles. You heal the blind, the lame, the scarred and leprous, the demon-possessed. You crack open prison cells, turn night into day, and roll the ocean up like a scroll. You send down fire from heaven. You bring the dead back to life. I am no Elijah, Lord, but I know You love me. Please answer my prayer today. Work my small miracle. Amen.

Then the fire of the LORD fell and consumed the burnt sacrifice, and the wood and the stones and the dust, and it licked up the water that was in the trench.

1 KINGS 18:38 NKJV

The Watcher

◆————————————————◆

Lord, I'm scared. I'm scared of someone I love getting sick. I'm scared of not having enough money. I'm scared of our country falling apart. I'm scared of being abandoned. I'm scared of hurting the ones I love. I'm scared of stepping on snakes. I'm scared of being laughed at. I'm scared that I'll grow old and die before You return. But mostly I'm scared of never knowing You better than I know You right now. Thank You for that fear, Lord, and how it drives me to my knees again and again. Amen.

The LORD will keep you from all harm—he will watch over your life; the LORD will watch over your coming and going both now and forevermore.

PSALM 121:7–8 NIV

Praying Like Breath

◆━━━━━━━◆

Lord, You gave me life, and I praise You. You filled my lungs with air from my very first breath, and I praise You. I praise You because I am fearfully and wonderfully made. Forgive me for not always loving this body You have given me like the amazing creation and great gift that it is. Today, Lord, I want to pray to You like I breathe: in and out, all day long. Fill my mouth with Your praise. Let my lips always be whispering Your name. Let my heart beat to the rhythm of Your perfect will. Amen.

Rejoice always; pray without ceasing.

1 THESSALONIANS 5:16–17 NASB

Call to Me

Lord of the universe, You know everything; You see everything; You are everywhere; You are every *time* and eternal. Lord, sometimes we think that we are so smart, we people that You *made*. Compared to You, we are babies, one minute old, looking up at the light and blinking, unable to comprehend anything. But You want us to grow up, Lord. You long to teach us everything You know. I yield my heart and mind to You. Amen.

"Call to me and I will answer you and tell you great and unsearchable things you do not know."

JEREMIAH 33:3 NIV

He Will Empower You
with Inner Strength

*If you were tied to the radio antenna at the top of
the Empire State Building with a very large gorilla
breathing down your neck, who would you be hoping to
see arrowing toward you out of the clouds? Superman?
Batman? Spiderman? Wonder Woman? The Bionic Man?
The Marlboro Man? One of these characters might get you
out of your temporary jam, but the next time the gorilla
grabbed you, you'd be just as helpless as before.
Those superheroes have strength, but none to share.
Jesus Christ, however, heads the pantheon because
He offers to share His power. He created the universe,
conquered death, compressed infinity to the size of a
human embryo, and defeated all the powers of evil.
And He offers us, according to the riches of His glory,
to be strengthened with that same might through
His Spirit. Some superhero, our God!*

Make Me Wiser

Dear Father, today I stumbled up against something that calls for Your wisdom. Someone might be in trouble, Lord. But it's a delicate situation, and I might be wrong. I've been wrong before, You know, and stepped out to offer help without Your blessing and just made things worse. I want to be used by You in people's lives, but first I need Your wisdom. I'm no Solomon, Lord, but just like he did, I'm asking for Your wisdom. Thank You that You promise to give it to me freely and generously. And please protect the woman with the bruised cheek. Amen.

If any of you lacks wisdom, let him ask of God, who gives to all liberally and without reproach, and it will be given to him.

JAMES 1:5 NKJV

The Salvation of Everyone!

Dear God, sometimes I get weary waiting for You. I am not patient about waiting for the things I long for with all my heart. But I know You are patient, Lord. You are waiting. You are waiting for *us*. Oh, thank You, that You won't return until everyone has had a chance to hear the Gospel. Thank You that Your incredible patience and love are greater than our persistent sin. Who can I tell, Lord? Who is near me who hasn't yet heard or understood the good news? Even so, come, Lord Jesus. Amen.

For I am not ashamed of the gospel of Christ:
for it is the power of God unto salvation
to every one that believeth.

Romans 1:16 KJV

The Cheerleader

Dear Lord, in this verse I can hear You cheering me on. What can I do? *All things!* Who's going to help me? *Christ!* What's He going to do? *Strengthen me!* I praise You for bringing these particular words to me right now. Your Word is so amazing: written thousands of years ago, yet it speaks to us perfectly in our moment of need. What other book is like that? What other god speaks to his people like You do? I know I am going to need this verse today, Lord. Help me to sing it back to You all day long. Amen.

I can do all things through Christ who strengthens me.

PHILIPPIANS 4:13 NKJV

The Construction Site

God, I am a work in progress. Sometimes I feel like there should be a barrier of construction tape and a hedge of warning signs up around all my rough edges. I am not who I want to be yet, Lord, and I know I'm not who *You* want me to be. Yet (and this is such a huge relief and amazement) You love me anyway. Thank You for Your mercy today and always and for the sure promise that You *are* carrying out Your work in me. Give me fertile soil and a yielding heart. Amen.

Being confident of this, that he who began
a good work in you will carry it on to
completion until the day of Christ Jesus.

PHILIPPIANS 1:6 NIV

If I Can?!

God, You are so amazing! When You first saved me, I suddenly felt like the world had shifted under me, and anything was possible. Even simple, mundane things such as breathing, eating, and looking up at the sky were made new. The knowledge that You did miracles (and might for me too) made me feel like I was standing on the edge of a new kind of life that was so beautiful and grand I might explode with joy. But it's not just a feeling, Lord. Anything *can* happen. I praise You with open wonder. Amen.

Jesus said, "If? There are no 'ifs' among believers. Anything can happen."

MARK 9:23 MSG

The Rock

Dear Father, I have a recurring skeptic in my life. He won't give up or give in, and nothing I say seems to make any difference in his opinion of You or Your Word. He's clinging to nothingness like a limpet on a rock, and I can't pull him off. Lord, I am weary of this fight, and I want to give up. But I know I am here because You put me here with this stubborn mollusk (whom You love). Please give me the strength to keep trying, lovingly and gently, to pry him loose from the big lie he is holding on to. You are the only rock. Amen.

For the Word that God speaks is alive and full of power. . .it is sharper than any two-edged sword, penetrating to the dividing line of the breath of life (soul) and [the immortal] spirit.

HEBREWS 4:12 AMPC

Who Are Your Philistines?

◆————————————◆

I am not a warrior, Lord. I am a weak woman. You know how many push-ups I can do, how many miles I can run, how long I can go without rest. But I have enemies too. Enemies of anger, self-control, discontent, cake, pride, selfishness, laziness. Strengthen me today for my battles against these foes. You are my high commander, Lord. Strengthen me with Your Spirit so I will be able to resist the enemy of my soul and follow only You. Amen.

"The LORD will cause your enemies who rise against you to be defeated before your face; they shall come out against you one way and flee before you seven ways."

DEUTERONOMY 28:7 NKJV

Groaning

Dear Lord, my heart and my mind feel empty right now. I don't know how to pray. I don't know what to pray. I just feel like a great weight is sitting on my chest, and I'm afraid the only thing that's going to come out is a horrible noise filled with tears and tiredness. Oh, Father. Thank You that You know I am weak and wordless. Thank You for Your Spirit, my comforter. Speak for me. Amen.

So too the [Holy] Spirit comes to our aid and bears us up in our weakness; for we do not know what prayer to offer nor how to offer it worthily as we ought, but the Spirit Himself goes to meet our supplication and pleads in our behalf with unspeakable yearnings and groanings too deep for utterance.

ROMANS 8:26 AMPC

In Temptation

Dear God, I'm trying to say no. Actually I'm trying to say no to this thing You've asked me to stop doing, and I'm trying to say no to You, at the same time. I don't want to be double-minded, both asking and doubting: I want Your blessing. So, Lord, help me with my temptation. Other people have struggled with exactly what I am struggling with. It is nothing new, only new to me. But You promise in Your Word that I am strong enough. Help me believe and not doubt. Amen.

No test or temptation that comes your way is beyond the course of what others have had to face. All you need to remember is that God will never let you down; he'll never let you be pushed past your limit; he'll always be there to help you come through it.

1 CORINTHIANS 10:13 MSG

At Your Nail-Torn Feet

—◆—◆—

Lord, thank You for the story of Ruth. I love the picture You paint with Boaz, the kinsman-redeemer, and how he rescued a hungry refugee girl and gave her the love, prosperity, and hope she was lacking. And thank You that when You describe Ruth and Boaz, You are also talking about me and my Savior. Since I am Your child, that means Jesus is my kinsman-redeemer too. I throw myself at Your feet, Jesus. Cover me with Your garment of grace. Live in me. Amen.

I have been crucified with Christ and I no longer live,
but Christ lives in me. The life I now live in the body,
I live by faith in the Son of God, who loved
me and gave himself for me.

GALATIANS 2:20 NIV

39

Jesus, in My Heart

Lord, sometimes I think of how the disciples must have felt after they watched You ascend into heaven: bereft, terrified, rootless. You had been everything to them, and suddenly You were gone. *What now?* they must have wondered. But forty days later, You were back. Not just for a visit but to *live* in them forever. Lord, You promise never to leave me or forsake me, and because of the great gift of Your Spirit, I know I am not alone. Thank You that You have made Your home in my heart. Amen.

And I will ask the Father, and He will give
you another Comforter (Counselor, Helper,
Intercessor, Advocate, Strengthener, and Standby),
that He may remain with you forever.

JOHN 14:16 AMPC

In Quietness

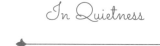

Lord, sometimes it feels like I never sit down. There are always so many things to do: people to manage, dishes to wash, bills to pay, groceries to buy, toilets to plunge, emails to answer. The noise and busyness of my life seem unending. But I know You call me to come away, just as Jesus did, and come to You in quietness and rest. Not just because You desire it, but because that quietness and rest in Your presence is the source of my strength. Thank You for longing to protect my heart in this crazy, merry-go-round world. Amen.

For thus saith the Lord GOD, the Holy One of Israel;
In returning and rest shall ye be saved; in quietness
and in confidence shall be your strength.

ISAIAH 30:15 KJV

Face to Grace

Father, my friend who loves You is dying. Her body is a minefield of cancer; the doctor says she has just weeks to live. Just a few weeks until she sees You face-to-face! But I praise You, Lord, in the midst of my tears because the power of Christ is so visibly resting on her right now, as she stands with her face touching the veil, seeing shadows of the next life. Only You can do this: give a woman, wasting away and saying goodbye to her young family, a joy and strength that evangelizes *others*. Even if You don't heal her, she is giving You all the glory. And I am seeing Your wonders. Amen.

And He said to me, "My grace is sufficient for you, for My strength is made perfect in weakness." Therefore most gladly I will rather boast in my infirmities, that the power of Christ may rest upon me.

2 Corinthians 12:9 nkjv

Strength in Joy

So often, Lord, I walk around with a glum face, as if being a child of the only living God weren't something to cheer about every moment of every day. I complain about how much work I have to do, how little I am appreciated, how relentlessly hard life seems sometimes. But You tell me in this verse to do these things: eat something yummy (thanks, Lord!), drink, share with others. Since Jesus came to earth, every day is a celebration. And Your festival-joy is the strength I need to keep on. Amen.

Nehemiah said, "Go and enjoy choice food and sweet drinks, and send some to those who have nothing prepared. This day is holy to our Lord. Do not grieve, for the joy of the LORD is your strength."

NEHEMIAH 8:10 NIV

In a Dry Time

---✦---

Dear Father, I want to pray, Lord, because You are beautiful and I love You, but the words will not come. I am dry and thirsty. But You are the living water, Jesus. You tell me in Your Word that if I come to You, streams of living water will flow from within me. Thank You for that promise. I am assured that this dry time will not last if I am faithful to come to You for refreshing. I am waiting on You.

On the last and greatest day of the festival, Jesus stood and said in a loud voice, "Let anyone who is thirsty come to me and drink. Whoever believes in me, as Scripture has said, rivers of living water will flow from within them."

JOHN 7:37–38 NIV

Christ Will Make His
Home in Your Heart

The cuckoo is an odd bird. Insect eaters, tree dwellers, some species are what is known as brood parasites, which means the adult cuckoo lays its single egg in another bird's nest. The baby cuckoo hatches before the host's eggs and pushes out the other chicks as they hatch. The unsuspecting host parents, designed to feed an open, squawking mouth, do just that, even though their "offspring" is the wrong color and bigger than they are. Sometimes we worry what Jesus will throw out when we ask Him to make His home in our hearts. Will we suddenly be clutching at precious things as they fall past us, out of reach? But He isn't like the cuckoo. He doesn't resort to trickery to get inside: He stands at the door and knocks. And once inside, He gently suggests how to renovate our hearts then gives us the desire and the will to do it.

Dinner at Jesus' House

Dear Father, I am so blessed that You continue to mold and shape me into the likeness of Your Son. Your Word says that Jesus didn't really have a home of His own. His home was wherever on the road He happened to be when night fell. But today, it hit me that my home, this walled place with bedrooms and tables and bathrooms, really is Jesus' home too. I ask Your blessing, Lord, as I seek to understand what that kind of house is like. I ask for Your grace and power to be real in our lives, *here.* Amen.

"Behold, I stand at the door and knock; if anyone hears My voice and opens the door, I will come in to him and will dine with him, and he with Me."

REVELATION 3:20 NASB

Unwrapping Jesus

It's dark, Lord, before the dawn on Your birthday. I can imagine what this dawn was like two thousand years ago. Mary and Joseph had been up all night, laboring on the straw, exhausted and filthy and terrified. Were You born at sunrise? We celebrate Your birth now with tinsel, decorated trees, and toys. But You came with blood and tears and terror. My children will be awake soon, Lord, and I want this day to be different than it usually is. Help me show them how the gift of Jesus outshines and outlasts all the glitter. Amen.

But the gift is not like the trespass. For if the many died by the trespass of the one man, how much more did God's grace and the gift that came by the grace of the one man, Jesus Christ, overflow to the many!

Romans 5:15 niv

49

Trail Signs

Dear God, I just want to thank You for speaking to me through another believer and keeping me from sin. Lord, You know how I longed to send that email and share something I shouldn't have. I was about to gossip, and I'm sorry. I'm so glad You sent someone to stand behind me and read over my shoulder and gently tell me not to hit SEND. Amen.

Your ears shall hear a word behind you, saying, "This is the way, walk in it," whenever you turn to the right hand or whenever you turn to the left.

ISAIAH 30:21 NKJV

Jesus Lives Here

＊——————————＊

Dear Jesus, You loved visiting Mary and Martha. Their house must have been a place of comfort, rest, and welcome for You. I wish I could sit at Your feet like Mary did, but then I realize that when I open Your Word, I am. Make my heart welcoming too, Lord, not a place of sharp corners, cobwebs, and hidden sins. Throw open the windows and let Your light shine in and out. Amen.

"Martha, Martha," the Lord answered, "you are worried and upset about many things, but few things are needed— or indeed only one. Mary has chosen what is better, and it will not be taken away from her."

LUKE 10:41–42 NIV

Before the Doorbell Rings

Dear Lord, I so wanted to have some quiet moments with You this morning. But the baby woke up early, the plumber called to say he's on his way, and the day is rushing at me down the tracks like a train. But I am going to choose joy today, Lord. I am going to choose to take what You give with open arms. I can pray where I stand, as I walk and talk; I can meditate on Your Word in any and every situation. And maybe I can get up earlier tomorrow! Amen.

All the days of the afflicted are evil, but he who is of a merry heart has a continual feast.

Proverbs 15:15 NKJV

Who Holds the Reins?

Dear Father, I spend so much time trying to control others. Futilely. I feel my anxiety mounting, and I know that is not what You want. I can only control my own heart, Lord, and that is only because of Your grace and the gift of Your Spirit. I can't be the "holy spirit" of anyone else's heart. That is Your job. Please help me let go of my agenda and instead lift others up to You. Work on and through *me*, Lord, so they would be drawn closer to You. Amen.

All the ways of a man are pure in his own eyes, but the Lord weighs the spirits. Commit your works to the Lord, and your thoughts will be established.

Proverbs 16:2–3 nkjv

Clean House

◆━━━━━━━━━◆

Dear God, my house is so messy. I just don't seem to have time to get the cobwebs off the ceiling or clean the drips off the fronts of the cabinets or scrub the smudges off the walls around the light switches. Please help me be content with imperfection because sometimes it seems like I can either clean or read Your Word, but not both. And I know it is far more important to wash the house of my soul with Your living water. Amen.

So that He might sanctify her, having cleansed her by the washing of water with the Word.

Ephesians 5:26 ampc

The Lord Is in the House

Dear Jesus, sometimes I imagine that You are in my house, sitting and watching our activities from the couch like a well-beloved guest. Thank You, Lord, that You care enough to come and stay. God's perfection is blinding and searing and annihilating, and if not for You, Jesus, we would die of it. You are holy (and wholly different) but still a man. I praise You, Jesus, for the sweetness of Your fellowship and the surprising ways You teach us to love. Amen.

But when the kindness and love of God our Savior appeared, he saved us, not because of righteous things we had done, but because of his mercy. He saved us through the washing of rebirth and renewal by the Holy Spirit.

TITUS 3:4–5 NIV

Words, Words, Words

Dear Father, my life is so full of words: books, TV, movies, neighbors, family, friends, letters, email, advertisements, radio. I am bombarded by them (and bombard others with mine) all day long, and I wonder how many of them really glorify You. And that *is* my desire, Lord: to glorify You. Please help me filter from the filth and froth what is pure and gracious. Help me desire truly to drink only Your pure milk so that it would flow out through me. Amen.

As newborn babes, desire the pure milk of the word,
that you may grow thereby, if indeed you have
tasted that the Lord is gracious.

1 Peter 2:2–3 nkjv

House Calls

Dear Lord, I find myself obsessing over certain people who upset me, like I'm picking at scabs. I think about how they have wounded me, and those wounds become deeper and sadder. Lord, when I do this, I am pushing Jesus out. I am not letting Him come into these situations and offer His gifts of forgiveness and healing. Please forgive me for relishing my wounds more than Your healing. Help me pray *for* people instead of muttering against them. I want to know You, Lord, and the power of Your resurrection, even in my small hurts. Amen.

He heals the brokenhearted and
binds up their wounds.

PSALM 147:3 NASB

Joy School

Joy is not my native language, Lord. I am more fluent in complaint, agitation, and bitterness. But this tongue of lead is heavy and wearying. I long to speak like the angels at the dawn of creation when they all shouted for joy! This is what I would say: You are good! You are holy! You are God! Those are the words that people are dying to hear. Thank You that I am made in Your image, so I can grow and change. I am not an animal, bound by my nature; I can learn another tongue. Amen.

"Come to Me, all who are weary and heavy-laden, and I will give you rest. Take My yoke upon you and learn from Me, for I am gentle and humble in heart, and you will find rest for your souls."

MATTHEW 11:28–29 NASB

Heart Transplant

Dear Father, You have blessed me with a healthy body, and I praise You for it. I have aches and pains and odd cramps and mysterious rumblings, but I've never had any broken bones, stitches, or spent the night in a hospital for anything except tonsils and childbirth! Thank You, Father. Many are not so blessed. But we all have hidden wounds, Father, wounds that bleed out onto other people. You know what mine are, even better than I do. You are the great healer, Lord. You heal with a touch, with a word. You heal simply with Your presence. Show me my hurts, Lord, and heal them. Amen.

Therefore, if anyone is in Christ, the new creation has come: The old has gone, the new is here!

2 Corinthians 5:17 niv

Rest

Dear Lord, today is Sunday. Every day is Your day, but You set aside this one specifically for us, to rest and worship You. Rest does not come easily to me, Lord. I plan and work and *do*. Resting seems somehow self-indulgent and lazy. But Your thoughts toward me are numerous, and higher than mine. I don't know what I need, but You do. Plans will be made today; messes will be made. Help me decide what honors Your commandment best in each situation: doing or waiting. Help me make my home and heart places of rest and worship. Show me what that means to You. Amen.

"For in six days the LORD made the heavens and the earth, the sea, and all that is in them, and rested the seventh day. Therefore the LORD blessed the Sabbath day and hallowed it."

EXODUS 20:11 NKJV

Pray for Me

✦━━━━━━━━━━✦

Dear Lord, how many times have I told someone I would pray for them, then never did? Those were lies, Lord. Forgetting to pray is like leaving a wounded fellow soldier behind on the battlefield. Forgive me. But I need You to help me remember, Lord, for my mind is small and harried and easily overrun. I trust You to be my general and bring them to mind when the fighting is fiercest and the need is greatest. Help me keep my heart and ears open to Your commands. Amen.

The LORD thunders at the head of his army;
his forces are beyond number, and mighty
is the army that obeys his command.

JOEL 2:11 NIV

Right There with Me

Dear God, how many times have I gone to sleep with a problem weighing on my mind and woken up in the morning with a solution that seemed to appear out of nowhere as I slept. I realize now that those miraculous solutions come from You. Thank You, Lord, for counseling me in the night, for instructing me even when I am not aware of it. It comforts me to know that You are so intimately concerned with me, and that even when I don't see Your hand or hear Your voice, You are right there with me. Amen.

I will praise the LORD, who counsels me;
even at night my heart instructs me.

PSALM 16:7 NIV

Your Roots Will Grow
Down into His Love

Now this is a true story. A certain man lived on a dusty road and dreamed of screening his house behind a hedge of evergreens. He bought sixty-four small trees and planted them on a warm day in May, but as the sun beat down, the needles on the little trees turned brown and fell off. The man planted sixty-four more trees. It was July by then, and hot. The weeks passed, and the little trees turned as bare and brittle as old Christmas trees. What went wrong? you ask. Whether through ignorance or laziness, the man never gave any of those trees a drop of water. Their roots shriveled before they reached the wet depths that would sustain them through the heat. Similarly, God's Word is our water, nourishing us through periods of drought and temptation. But water does nothing in a bucket or on a shelf. Open it up, pour it out, drink.

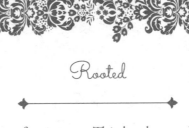

Rooted

◆————————◆

Lord, please forgive me. This has been a hard time, and I have been entertaining doubts of all sorts. I am just realizing, as I sit here in the quiet with You, that I was under attack and I parleyed with the enemy. I see how the attack went, now: first pride, then a judging spirit, then self-doubt, then bitterness, then despair, then an existential doubt of the most foul sort. *Do You love me? Are You really there?* I long to grow deep, Lord. I am tired of being torn out by the roots over and over. Give me the diligence I am lacking to grow deep in You, down through streams of living water to the solid Rock. Amen.

A man is not established by wickedness,
but the root of the righteous cannot be moved.

Proverbs 12:3 NKJV

Deeper

How much is enough, Lord? How deep is deep enough? I read once that the deepest tree roots ever recorded went down well over one hundred feet. I want to be that deep in You. I want the energy of my growth to go downward, not to attractive but weak side branches that just sap my strength. Show me what I need to prune from my life, Lord. Make me willing to clip and snip and shape. Lord, I'm sure Paul's good looks were marred by the beatings, imprisonment, snakebites, and shipwrecks he endured for Your sake, but how firmly he stood! Help me value a firm, rooted faith more than pretty flowers and a pleasing appearance. Amen.

They have bowed down and fallen;
but we have risen and stand upright.

PSALM 20:8 NKJV

Stronger

Lord, You know this is a difficult season in my life. When I was younger, You staked and sheltered me like a precious sapling, but now I am faced with stresses that I never imagined before. Sickness, grief, aging, loss, hardship. Yet I stand. I am amazed at the strength You are giving me daily. Lord, I know myself, and I *know* this is all from You. All these things You are using for Your glory. I know I won't look back from heaven at the events of my life and say anything other than *hallelujah*. I am saying it now. *Hallelujah. Hallelujah.*

> *And we know that all things work together*
> *for good to them that love God, to them who*
> *are the called according to his purpose.*

ROMANS 8:28 KJV

Taller

+————————————+

Dear good, gracious heavenly Father, sometimes it is so dark here. Not just the darkness of night or storm or interiors: the darkness of sin and unknowing presses close. I am reaching up for Your light in the only way I can. Thank You, Lord, for Your Word. It comforts and illuminates in a way that nothing else does. It makes You present and real to me. I praise You for giving me something that is so *alive* with Your Spirit to be my anchor and lantern in the darkness. Amen.

The entrance and unfolding of Your words give light;
their unfolding gives understanding (discernment
and comprehension) to the simple.

PSALM 119:130 AMPC

69

Seedlings

Dear Father, I know my children give You as much joy as they give me, and I just want to thank You for them today. Thank You for their quick minds, their healthy bodies, their loving hearts, their hilarious antics. Most of the time I'm so busy feeding, teaching, disciplining, and organizing them that I don't take even a moment to praise You for what awesome creations they are. Each unique and precious, and each with a soul that will live forever. Give me grace as I continue to point their hearts to You. Amen.

And he took the children in his arms,
placed his hands on them and blessed them.

MARK 10:16 NIV

Transplanted

Dear God, You know I am about to move, *again*. Even though this is a move I've been waiting, hoping, and longing for, it will still be stressful. Please be with me in this transition. Amid all the plans and packing, I pray that You would help keep my eyes focused on You. No matter where I put down roots for the next year, or ten or twenty, my true home is in heaven and my true roots in Christ alone. Amen.

Instead, they were longing for a better country—
a heavenly one. Therefore God is not ashamed to be
called their God, for he has prepared a city for them.

HEBREWS 11:16 NIV

Weeds

Dear Lord, You are the Master Gardener. I love to plant flowers, vegetables, bushes, and bulbs, but nothing in my garden can compare with the glory that was Eden. Every plant, tiny or large, was deliberately placed to bring delight to Adam's and Eve's eyes, and not a weed marred the smooth perfection of soil and grass. My garden is nothing like that: if I ignore it for two weeks, weeds spring up; in two months it would be a jungle. My life is just like my garden, Lord. Sometimes new things seem insignificant at first: a new TV program, a new book, a new acquaintance, a new train of thought. But they can grow rampantly. Give me wisdom to recognize weeds when they are small and pluck them out. Amen.

For wisdom is better than rubies, and all the things one may desire cannot be compared with her.

PROVERBS 8:11 NKJV

Rootstock

Dear Father, You are a God who is faithful from generation to generation. Thank You for the men and women in my family tree who loved You and passed a godly heritage down to my parents and to me. I praise You that You are the same yesterday, today, and tomorrow: You are the same God that Abraham worshipped four thousand years ago, that Paul worshipped two thousand years ago, that my great-grandfather worshipped one hundred years ago. And I praise You that my children and their children's children can follow the same unchanging God. Amen.

Know therefore that the LORD your God is God;
he is the faithful God, keeping his covenant of love to
a thousand generations of those who love
him and keep his commandments.

DEUTERONOMY 7:9 NIV

Watered

Dear Father, I thank You for things that reach upward, that remind me to lift my arms in praise. Mountains, trees, clouds—they all reach higher than my little arms, but only I can praise You. When I praise You, Lord, I feel so different: washed clean with joy and somehow taller. I feel like a plant after a spring rain. I praise You for the beauty of the earth, the skies, and the heavens, and for Your great love, which surrounds and sustains it all. Amen.

He dawns on them like the morning light when the sun rises on a cloudless morning, when the tender grass springs out of the earth through clear shining after rain.

2 SAMUEL 23:4 AMPC

Wilder

Dear God, today I ask You for strength. I need Your strength to break old habits of sin that are holding me back from the freedom You promise me in Christ. The devil wants me tame: a creature fully at his bidding. Only You, God, give me the capacity to grow and change and stretch. I ask for Your courage today as I abandon old patterns and step past the borders of what is easy and familiar into the wild, beautiful country beyond. Help me to trust that, even if it looks like I am the only one following this path, You are guiding me every step of the way. Amen.

By faith Abraham obeyed when he was called to go out to the place which he would receive as an inheritance. And he went out, not knowing where he was going.

Hebrews 11:8 nkjv

Staked

Lord, the wind is howling like a beast around the house right now. Everything that is not nailed down tight rattles and moans. Our house can stand this much wind, Lord, but how much *more* before it whirls away? Sometimes, Lord, when the wind howls so and reminds me of my frailty, I wonder how long *I* can hold on. How many more tragedies, trials, and temptations? But then You are there, beloved Savior, reminding me of the everlasting arms that are always around me, comforting, sustaining, and protecting. Thank You, Jesus. I stake my life on You. Amen.

The eternal God is your refuge and dwelling place,
and underneath are the everlasting arms.

DEUTERONOMY 33:27 AMPC

Nourished

Dear Father, I thank You for Your church. I have worshipped You and listened to teaching from Your Word in so many different buildings, but the same Spirit has filled them. I know I could walk into any Bible-believing church in Seoul, Zanzibar, Toledo, or Des Moines and feel immediately at home. That is because You are there too. I thank You for the church I am a part of right now. I pray that You would bless all the people who serve there with extra measures of Your joy, strength, and love this week. Amen.

There are different kinds of gifts, but the same Spirit distributes them. There are different kinds of service, but the same Lord. There are different kinds of working, but in all of them and in everyone it is the same God at work.

1 Corinthians 12:4–6 niv

Gardening

◆————————————◆

Dear Lord, other people's lives can be so messy. Like a teenager's room, it's tempting to close the door and ignore what is inside. But You are a God who is not afraid of messes. You are not afraid to reach into the tangles and the mire. You see into the future of a lost person's heart: You see a garden where I only see a dangerous wilderness where *I* might get hurt—or simply dirty. Lord, I want to be like You; I want to love the lost like You do. Help me to look past the mess to the eternal soul inside. Amen.

For the Son of man is come to seek
and to save that which was lost.

LUKE 19:10 KJV

Harvest

Dear Lord, I thank You that the other night a little girl I love prayed in the dark with her older sister to ask You into her heart. I thank You that other children are asking their friends from school to come to youth group and that they are getting *saved*. I thank You for the teenagers of a dear friend who love You more than anything in their lives. I thank You for a girl who prays for her grandmother's salvation every day. Lord, the fields are white unto harvest, and You are lifting up faithful laborers even among the little ones. Amen.

For this is good and acceptable in the sight of God our Savior, who desires all men to be saved and to come to the knowledge of the truth.

1 Timothy 2:3–4 nkjv

Birdsong

Lord, I praise You for the little birds in my garden: the chickadees, the robins, the juncos, the purple finches. I praise You for the evening song of the hermit thrush. They are like sequins on a glorious world! You've thought of everything, Lord, and You rejoice in it. Help me remember that as much as I rejoice in songbirds, You rejoice in me even more. Because I am of more value than many sparrows. But thank You for the sparrows too. Amen.

"The LORD your God in your midst, the Mighty One, will save; He will rejoice over you with gladness, He will quiet you with His love, He will rejoice over you with singing."

ZEPHANIAH 3:17 NKJV

Understanding the Width,
Length, Height, and Depth
of His Love

The size of the universe is a question that invites much debate among scientists. Some say it's twenty billion light-years across and still expanding; others say it's considerably smaller. But the bottom line is it's really, really big. Jesus knows about volume. As the son of a carpenter, Jesus was comfortable with calculations. He knew the amount of wood to use to build a box that would hold an ephah of barley. He knew what size house a certain amount of wood could build. And as God and Creator, He knows the exact dimensions of the universe. Understanding the volume of God's love is not just a question of length times width times height. There is another variable—time—because God's love stretches from before the foundations of the world, through history, and into eternity. And when time is multiplied in, God's love becomes incalculably large.

Googolplex

Lord, You are infinite and beyond comprehension. I *know* this with my head, but infinity is such a nonhuman sort of concept! I try to think about You in this way, but my mind keeps trying to reduce You to something smaller, something I can wrap my understanding around. I praise You that You are wholly infinite and infinitely holy. Who is like You? I don't understand, but I rest, a speck in Your loving hand. Amen.

He telleth the number of the stars; he calleth them all by their names. Great is our Lord, and of great power: his understanding is infinite.

Psalm 147:4–5 KJV

Grace in the Not-Knowing

◆———————◆

Lord, tonight I've cried and cried, and You've listened and loved me and given me words of truth and comfort. But I'm still confused. Someone I love is with You tonight. This morning she was with her husband and children. I wonder why You didn't heal her, because I know You could have and I thought You were going to! Why, Lord? I don't know how to rejoice that she is walking on streets of gold and at the same time weep that her children will grow up without her. But I rest in Your sovereignty, Lord. Please help me live with grace in the not-knowing. Amen.

So when. . .this mortal has put on immortality,
then shall be brought to pass the saying that is
written: "Death is swallowed up in victory."

1 CORINTHIANS 15:54 NKJV

The Rescue

Dear Father, tonight I watched a movie in which a sweet but foolish girl was kidnapped and sold into slavery in a foreign country. No one would help her, except her father, who crashed through every barrier and mowed down every bad guy who stood in his way. Though stabbed, beaten, and broken, he found her and rescued her and brought her home. I just started weeping, Father, when I realized that *this* is exactly what You have done for me. I was lost and alone and sold into slavery in this sin-stricken world. You *came*. You rescued me. Thank You, again and again. Amen.

> *"He rescues and he saves; he performs signs*
> *and wonders in the heavens and on the earth."*
>
> DANIEL 6:27 NIV

Crocuses

Dear Lord, I just want to praise You today for the surprising ways You love us. Thank You for the way rain droplets spangle a branch like diamonds. Thank You for a stranger's unexpected smile in a busy store. Thank You for the pictures You paint every evening at sunset. Thank You for clear, rushing streams and cold drinks of water. Thank You for the bright heads of crocuses that spring out of the dregs of winter. Thank You for how You delight in surprising me with the beauty of Your Word and Your world. Amen.

For the LORD thy God bringeth thee into a good land, a land of brooks of water, of fountains and depths that spring out of valleys and hills.

DEUTERONOMY 8:7 KJV

The Terrible Mercy

◆————————◆

Dear Lord, I just finished thanking You for the little moments of beauty You gift me with every day. Then, suddenly, as the sunset faded, the horror of this world seemed to hit me along with the darkness. There are crocuses and raindrops and smiles but also broken bones and broken marriages, breast lumps and biopsies, wars and widows. It's so hard to know what to do with all this beauty so inextricably mixed up with all this viciousness. I am crying out to You. Help me trust Your love even as I try to understand it, Lord. Amen.

"Though he slay me, yet will I hope in him."

Job 13:15 niv

Holes

Dear Lord, You know where I was when You found me: at the bottom of a hole so deep even the end of my rope was out of reach. All I wanted to do was pull the dirt down on my own head and die. But You didn't let me. And You didn't just reach down to me; You jumped *in*. Verses, people, hymns, moments of unexpected beauty—they all showed me that You were right there with me, loving me, lifting me. Thank You for changing the ending of my story, Lord, and giving me a tale to tell to the lost. Thank You for the transformative power of Your love. Amen.

He also brought me up out of a horrible pit. . . .
He has put a new song in my mouth—praise to our God;
many will see it and fear, and will trust in the LORD.

PSALM 40:2–3 NKJV

Warming My Hands by Holy Fire

Dear Lord, it's so cold this morning. Frost covers the ground, and the air is as still as ice. My fingers are cold too, but I thank You for a warm cup of tea and a house with a furnace. You always provide for me and protect me, Lord. I never need worry. Thank You that Your love doesn't wax and wane like the warmth of the sun through the seasons. You are a constant and faithful source of light and warmth for my soul. Don't let me grow cold, Lord, but keep my hands pressed up against Your blaze. Amen.

For our God is a consuming fire.

HEBREWS 12:29 NKJV

Little Creaks down the Stairs

Dear Father, I can't count how many times I've just sat down at my desk with my Bible and a cup of coffee when I hear the telltale, hesitant creaks on the stairs indicating the approach of a small person who isn't sure of his reception. I confess, Lord, that my heart sinks. But I want more than anything to be like You, and I know that there is never a time when I reach out to You and Your heart doesn't *leap*. I want my children—and the other people around me—to understand the depth of Your love. Help me show them, in part, through the depth of *my* love for them. Amen.

But it is good for me to draw near to God:
I have put my trust in the Lord GOD,
that I may declare all thy works.

PSALM 73:28 KJV

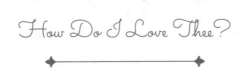

How Do I Love Thee?

Dear God, *love* is such a little word, just four letters—a greeting card, fairy-tale, romance novel word. I say I love hamburgers with the same verb I would use to say I love Jesus. Most of the time I don't think about the power of that word: how it can move mountains, calm storms, heal lepers, redeem a sinner. That word saved me from hell. I remember when I first fell in love, how I longed to hear that word back from my beloved. And that earthly love is just a dim shadow of what You feel for me. I love You, Lord. Let me never stop counting the ways. Amen.

"For God so loved the world that He gave His only begotten Son, that whoever believes in Him should not perish but have everlasting life."

JOHN 3:16 NKJV

In the Neighborhood

Dear Father, I am surrounded on all sides by people who are dangerously close to spending eternity without You. They are one misstep (a fall off a ladder, a stumble into traffic) from an eternity they cannot even imagine. I would run into the road to stop a man from being hit by a car; I would scream to wake a woman asleep in a blazing house. But when it's a question of eternity, I say nothing. Open my eyes, Lord, to the moments when the enemy's lying tongue is quiet, and give me Your words to say. You love them so much, Lord. They are just one *prayer* away from an eternity they cannot imagine. Amen.

Who is a God like You, who pardons iniquity and passes over the rebellious act of the remnant of His possession? He does not retain His anger forever, because He delights in unchanging love.

Micah 7:18 nasb

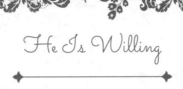

He Is Willing

Dear God, I am astounded by Your love! You love us so much that You were willing to leave Your kingly throne and come down into the muck and the sin. For a holy God, sin is *worse* than leprosy. You can't even look upon it. Yet Jesus did. I'm not a leper, *exactly*. My face isn't marred by open sores; I'm not missing pieces of my lips and nose. But sometimes my face *is* mottled by anger, and I'm missing large chunks of the love, joy, peace, patience, kindness, goodness, faithfulness, gentleness, and self-control that are my birthright in Christ. Again and again, You are willing to reach out and touch me and cleanse me with Your amazing love. Thank You, Jesus.

Jesus reached out his hand and touched the man. "I am willing," he said. "Be clean!" Immediately he was cleansed of his leprosy.

MATTHEW 8:3 NIV

The Promise Keeper

Dear Father, how many times have I promised (even just to myself) to call someone and didn't? How many times have I promised to play dolls with my little girl or read a story to my son and didn't? How many times have I promised to get a certain job done and didn't? Forgive me for breaking those promises. You are a God who keeps His promises, who is faithful from generation to generation. Teach me what it means to be truly faithful. Amen.

For no matter how many promises
God has made, they are "Yes" in Christ.

2 CORINTHIANS 1:20 NIV

The Eternal Security System

Dear Lord, Your Word says that we are protected, all unawares, by Your mighty angels. They accompany us and defend us and preserve us when we are walking in Your way. This is not just another security system with a little picture of an angel to stick in our front lawn to deter criminals; they don't just sound an alarm in heaven when our walls have been breached. They keep evil *away*. I know there have been times in my life when You protected me, and I was very aware of it. Thank You, Lord. Thank You also for the invisible guardians that surround me and defend me from the evil I never even see. Amen.

For He will give His angels [especial] charge over you to accompany and defend and preserve you in all your ways [of obedience and service].

PSALM 91:11 AMPC

Rule of Love

Dear Lord, You are Lord of the universe, yet You left Your throne and came down to earth to be near us. You are the giver and sustainer of life, yet You sacrificed Your Son to save us. You are the King of kings, yet You put aside Your crown to become one of us. There is no precedent for this kind of love. The president of the United States wouldn't sacrifice his child for peace in the Middle East or send his child to live with beggars in India so they could learn about democracy. That would never happen. What You did for us makes no earthly sense. But You did it, and I am forever grateful. Amen.

"To him who sits on the throne and to the Lamb be praise and honor and glory and power, for ever and ever!"

REVELATION 5:13 NIV

Mother's Day in January

✦

Dear Lord, I thank You today for my mother. No one else except You has loved me like she has. From before I was born, through sickness and rebellion, and even when I was thousands of miles away, she has loved me. You blessed me so much when You gave me to this particular woman. I praise You for her gentleness, generosity, and quiet strength. I pray that You would bless her today, Lord, with the awareness of how her love and Yours have made a difference in eternity. Amen.

"As one whom his mother comforts,
so I will comfort you."

Isaiah 66:13 nasb

You Will Be

Made Complete

Joanne clutched the writhing, convulsing girl in the back of the truck as it sped through the dark Thailand night. Rushing Khut to the hospital for what appeared to be an allergic reaction, it was becoming clear that something darker was at work. Joanne was on a two-week mission trip, and this wild ride with a demon-possessed girl was more than she had bargained for. How close can I be to darkness and not be swallowed up? *she wondered. The answer came immediately: nothing can separate you from the love of God. The doctor sedated Khut, but the next day it happened again. This time, it took three men to hold her down. One of them pleaded, "Just confess Jesus and you can be rid of this." She spit in his face and growled, "No." Pray for Khut. She is glaringly incomplete, and the missing piece in her heart is the shape of the cross.*

In Any and Every Situation

Dear Lord, right now my belly is full and my body is well rested, and I confess that I confuse that physical contentment with spiritual health. And at other times I have believed the lie that aches, pains, and sickness mean You have withdrawn Your hand of blessing from me. Neither is necessarily true, as You make abundantly clear in Your Word. Paul had a thorn in his flesh, while the healthy and wealthy You struck down. Conversely, demons caused sickness, and You blessed Solomon with great wealth. I am complete in Christ, regardless of my circumstances. Help me live in the light of eternity, unswayed by bank balances, buffets, or blood tests. Amen.

From the fruit of their mouth a person's stomach is filled;
with the harvest of their lips they are satisfied.

PROVERBS 18:20 NIV

Pascal's Puzzle

Dear Lord, someone once wrote that there is a God-shaped hole inside every person. I know I felt it, and tried to fill that hole with so many things besides You: work, school, achievement, friends, parties, travel. But nothing was a perfect fit, and the hole remained. But when You found me, even though in pride and fear I tried to say no, the piece that was missing clicked into place. I thank You, Lord, for that hole, for showing me that I was created for something different than a "normal" life. Stop me, Lord, if I lose my first love and start filling that hole with something besides You. Amen.

Once you were alienated from God. . . . But now he has reconciled you by Christ's physical body through death to present you holy in his sight, without blemish and free from accusation.

COLOSSIANS 1:21–22 NIV

At Dawn in Eden

Dear Father, I have always longed to be in the garden of Eden in those first days when You walked with Adam and Eve in the cool of the day. You enjoyed Your creation; You thought it was beautiful. You enjoyed Your creatures, especially Your people, and You wanted to spend time with them. I am so sorry for what we lost, and I know You are too. We lost the completeness we had in Eden: we lost that perfect garden and that perfect fellowship with You. But the gift is not like the trespass. Thank You that what You gave us in Jesus Christ is even more beautiful than what we lost. Amen.

And they heard the sound of the LORD God walking in the garden in the cool of the day.

GENESIS 3:8 NKJV

Semper Paratus

God, today I have felt like a concrete footing when the forms get removed. Am I dry and sturdy? Will I stand on my own? Will I support a structure above me? I confess that I've been depending on the faith and scripture knowledge of people around me instead of developing my own. When I stand before You, You aren't going to ask whether I was the cousin of a Bible scholar or married to a person of great faith. You will see *me*. I long to hear You say, "Well done." Increase my faith and devotion to You. Amen.

> *"But rise and stand on your feet;*
> *for I have appeared to you for this purpose,*
> *to make you a minister and a witness."*

ACTS 26:16 NKJV

Essential Jesus

◆————————◆

Lord, I see in myself the tendency to become a Pharisee: to add rules to the essential simplicity of the Gospel. Sometimes I wonder if maybe I need to dress differently, read only a certain translation of the Bible, talk with a more specialized "Christian" vocabulary. But then You remind me of Acts 16:31. Believe in the Lord Jesus. Be saved. That's it. It's not esoteric knowledge; it's not an unattainable level of enlightenment; it's not dressing a certain way; it's not a thousand-mile pilgrimage: it's just You, Jesus. Help me stay true to this message by staying close to You. Amen.

They replied, "Believe in the Lord Jesus, and you will be saved—you and your household."

ACTS 16:31 NIV

The Already-Done List

Dear God, I love plans and schedules. They help me stay focused and productive and turn the 1,440 minutes in each day into goals set and attained. But I know I have missed opportunities to deepen relationships because I was too busy checking off boxes on my to-do list or too rigid to change plans at the last minute. And I know that often I base my idea of how much *I* am worth on how much I have been able to accomplish. Help me remember that I can never *do* enough to earn Your love. I am already loved, completely and eternally. The only thing that really needed doing, You did on the cross. Thank You, Lord.

The LORD appeared to him from afar, saying,
"I have loved you with an everlasting love;
therefore I have drawn you with lovingkindness."

JEREMIAH 31:3 NASB

Cry in the Night

Dear Lord, there is never a time I cry out to You and You are not instantly listening. Unlike the false god of the prophets of Baal, You are never busy, traveling, sleeping, or too deep in thought to hear me. The only thing that stops my prayers from reaching You is my own unconfessed sin. Help me examine my heart when I fear that You are silent. Forgive my sins. I long to stand before You, complete and unashamed. Just as I run to my baby when he cries, I know I am never alone. Amen.

"Then you call on the name of your god,
and I will call on the name of the LORD.
The god who answers by fire—he is God."

1 KINGS 18:24 NIV

The Liar

Dear God, someone I care about told me a lie today—in church, no less. It was a small lie, about an insignificant thing, but it felt like a brick had been thrown at me. I carried that brick like an ugly goblin baby—a changeling—all through the service, and the music, the sermon, the fellowship of other believers were soured for me because of my burden. Then I realized, Lord, because You so lovingly showed me, that the burden had become mine because I chose to carry it. A small lie became in my heart the equal sin of anger, resentment, and despair. Thank You for showing me how to lay that ugly thing at the foot of the cross and pick up joy instead. Amen.

If we confess our sins, he is faithful and just to forgive us our sins, and to cleanse us from all unrighteousness.

1 JOHN 1:9 KJV

The One Needful Thing

Dear Father, You are the giver of good gifts, but I confess that I'm often on the lookout for more. I go to the store, Lord, and all the things I see look so nice and necessary. They are just sitting there on the shelves, but in my mind, they are jumping up and down, dancing, and waving to get my attention: *Hey, pick me! No, me! I'll make you happy! I'll make you thinner! Take me with you!* Thank You for the things I have, but help me control my desire for more. No *thing* I have will defile me, but neither will it make me complete. Only You can do that, Jesus. Amen.

I will be fully satisfied as with the richest of foods;
with singing lips my mouth will praise you.

PSALM 63:5 NIV

The Perfectionist Trap

Dear Lord, I am so glad that You are such a high, mighty, and separate God. I praise You that You are not like the gods of the Vikings or the Greeks, quarrelsome tricksters and schemers. We can only make gods in our own image. We could never imagine You, Lord. I would never bow to Artemis or Baal or Thor, but I realized just now in my perfectionism I am setting up another god to worship—myself. Always doing, striving, perfecting, tweaking my little universe. Please help me be content with imperfection. Only You are perfect, and I am complete, now, in You. Amen.

As for God, His way is perfect.

2 Samuel 22:31 AMPC

Fresh Ink

Dear Lord, I pray for insight today as I read Your Word. Open it to me, Lord, and reveal Your heart to me. I confess that it has not been my meat and drink as it should. I want to know You better today than I did yesterday, and better tomorrow than I do today. Thank You for the Holy Spirit, who guides me as I read, and I pray for a fresh filling of that Spirit. You make all things new, Lord, and I thank You for the verses I will read today and how they will speak to me, as if You wrote them for me this morning, as if the ink is still wet. Amen.

I lean on, rely on,
and trust in Your word.

PSALM 119:42 AMPC

Mirror, Mirror

Father, when I look at certain people I know, all I see is how much I lack in comparison. They seem naturally kinder, more at ease, more fashionable, more attractive, and certainly thinner. I know, Lord, I often spend more time thinking about how other people see me than about how You see me. You made me, sovereign Lord, in this particular way for Your purposes. Help me trust You and trust that this lump of clay that You are molding is precious in Your sight and in Your hands. Amen.

I will praise You, for I am fearfully
and wonderfully made.

PSALM 139:14 NKJV

Where's Your Missing Piece?

———◆———

Dear Lord, the people who still need You don't usually advertise it out loud. They don't usually go around with "unsaved" or "missing Jesus" emblazoned on their T-shirts. Sometimes they look just fine, like they aren't missing anything at all. Lord, this is when I feel most uncertain how to tell them about You. I need Your eyes, Lord, to see exactly where and how deep are their "God-shaped holes." Unbelievers are not complete, despite how they may appear. I trust You to lead me, for You love them so much. Amen.

In Him you have been made complete.

Colossians 2:10 nasb

My Prayer Warriors

I thank You, Lord, today for all the people who have prayed for me. I am humbled by how I have been surrounded, from the day I was born, by people who have lifted me up to the throne of grace, faithfully and passionately. I may not ever know who they are, but I ask You to bless them today. Strengthen their faith in the invisible power of their work. I ask that You would bring me to their minds today, Lord, for I covet their intercession. Thank You for these faithful warriors. I need them so desperately. Amen.

Always labouring fervently for you in prayers, that ye may stand perfect and complete in all the will of God.

COLOSSIANS 4:12 KJV

The Unveiling

◆————————◆

Lord, I'm wondering what it really means to be complete in Jesus Christ. What does *complete* really mean, for me? Whole. Absolute. Total. Finished. Accomplished. Concluded. Fulfilled. Done. These are all synonyms, and I am struck by their common sense of finality. There is nothing left to be done. My transformation from stone to flesh was finished at the cross. The work is done; we are just awaiting the final unveiling. Praise Jesus. Amen.

But we all, with unveiled face, beholding as in a mirror
the glory of the Lord, are being transformed into
the same image from glory to glory.

2 Corinthians 3:18 nasb

Your Life Will Be
Full and Powerful

On the afternoon of January 8, 2011, the stands at Qwest
Field in Seattle were packed with nearly 70,000 fans for
the game between the Seahawks and the Saints. Seattle
football fans have a reputation for being loud, and the
acoustics in the stadium are such that the sound is
trapped and amplified. This day was no exception.
The noise was deafening. Fans screamed, cheered,
and stomped so enthusiastically that a nearby seismometer
monitored by the Pacific Northwest Seismic Network
registered an earthquake. True, it was a small one:
only 1 or 2 on the Richter scale. But it was an earthquake.
The real game is almost over too: our quarterback,
Jesus Christ, is running into the end zone, ready to score
the last touchdown. And we already know that we
win. How loud is our love? Cheer. Stomp. Yell.
Just think how we can rock the world for Jesus.

The Well of Words

Lord, You've given me a love of words, and by Your grace, You've allowed me to use it. Sometimes, though, I worry that I'll run out of things to say. What if the well runs dry? But then I remember how You created everything out of nothing. You spoke, and it came to be. You are the author of life, the Word made flesh. Thank You for breathing that same spark of creativity into us along with the breath of life. I know that if I keep my eyes fixed on You, I'll never run out of words. There is no end to the ways I can praise You! Amen.

"Whoever drinks the water I give them will never thirst. Indeed, the water I give them will become in them a spring of water welling up to eternal life."

JOHN 4:14 NIV

Time Machine

Dear Lord, I have so much work to do each day and so little time. I always feel like I'm running behind. It's a treadmill, Lord, set on a speed that's just a little too fast for me to keep up; I'm always just on the verge of flying off the back into a heap on the floor. But I know this is not what You want. Jesus was a man who was never in a hurry. He had just enough time to do the Father's will. He had time to pray on a mountainside, time to chat beside a well, time to sit by a lake and cook a fish with friends. Give me wisdom as I seek to set aside my endless to-do list for Your holy will. Amen.

There is a time for everything, and a season for every activity under the heavens.

ECCLESIASTES 3:1 NIV

121

The Beacon

My family isn't perfect, Lord. You know how often selfishness, angry words, hurt feelings, and laziness mar our relationships with each other. You know how we are when the door is shut and no one is watching. But we love You, and You are teaching us to love. Increase our love: let it shine out for everyone around to see. Make us a light on a hill, Lord, so that those in darkness will see our Jesus. Amen.

No one has seen God at any time.
If we love one another, God abides in us,
and His love has been perfected in us.

1 JOHN 4:12 NKJV

Cobwebs of the Soul

Dear Father, You know how good I feel when my house is in order, when the floors are swept, the bathrooms are clean, the beds are made, and the toys are picked up. It imparts an order and peace to my soul. And You know how I feel when chaos reigns: scattered, bewildered, short-tempered. Help me remember that it is no different with my spiritual house. Help me keep the cobwebs and confusion in check with daily prayer, study, and meditation on Your Word. And thank You that I *can*. Amen.

> *You will keep him in perfect peace,*
> *whose mind is stayed on You.*
>
> ISAIAH 26:3 NKJV

Accountability

How many times, Lord, have I heard about Christian leaders who fell into great sin. I may have read their books, seen them on TV, and then suddenly their lives and ministries crumbled to bits when sin that was hidden came to light. Those leaders probably never imagined where their sin would take them, and I thank You for reminding me that I too am capable of any sin. Please protect me, Lord. Surround me with people who will ask tough questions about my life and hold me accountable. I want to be useful to You, Lord, not a broken object of scorn and pity. Amen.

The LORD will be at your side and will
keep your foot from being snared.

PROVERBS 3:26 NIV

A Dream Deferred Can Bloom

When I feel small and insignificant, Lord, You so graciously remind me of this verse. When I remember the goals and dreams I had when I was younger, which I have not achieved because I chose to follow You instead, You remind me where true worth lies. Thank You for the contentment that only comes from following You. But I thank You too for how You are fulfilling some of my old dreams in unexpected ways. I love You, and I trust You completely. If my heart is set on You, then what You give me *will* be the desire of my heart. Amen.

He hath made every thing beautiful in his time.

ECCLESIASTES 3:11 KJV

Disguises Off!

Lord, You have let me be part of the most amazing thing in the world—Your church. Where believers gather, You are present, and Your glory is made visible. I confess that often I don't even try to look with Your eyes. I see an old building, full of strange people doing odd things. I need to see with Your eyes: that our hundred-year-old church is really a shining fortress, that our creaky voices are a descant to the most glorious choral music in the universe, that the retired accountant in the pew behind me is really a warrior in brilliant armor. And I am something more than I appear. Help me retrain my eyes, Lord, to see as You do. Amen.

For now we see through a glass, darkly; but then
face to face: now I know in part; but then
shall I know even as also I am known.

1 CORINTHIANS 13:12 KJV

A Caged Bird Singing

Dear God, I want to thank You for Paul and Silas. Seized and hauled through the marketplace, stripped and beaten with rods, thrown into prison—they prayed and sang hymns from their jail cell. Your Word says the other prisoners were *listening* to them: listening and learning what it means to serve a risen Savior. Nothing like that has ever happened to me, Lord, and I am very grateful. I have never felt the terror of a mob; I have never felt the touch of an angry hand; I have never been in prison. My trials are ordinary. But I pray that even still, I would be faithful to praise You in them—because people are listening. Amen.

*Rejoice to the extent that you partake of Christ's
sufferings, that when His glory is revealed,
you may also be glad with exceeding joy.*

1 Peter 4:13 NKJV

The Proof Is in the Pudding

Dear Father, we are a gullible people. From the very beginning, we were tricked and led astray. Satan whispered in Eve's ear, she listened, and everyone ever since has been falling for his lies. *Just this once. It doesn't really matter. I deserve this. No one will find out.* We believe his lies about everything from eating too much chocolate, to "borrowing" a pencil from work, to committing adultery or murder. I am no different. I need You every moment, Lord, to help me sort through the chatter in my head so I can be certain what to listen to and what to stand against. Only the truth. Only what glorifies You. Amen.

"Then you will know the truth,
and the truth will set you free."

JOHN 8:32 NIV

Little Mary Quite Extraordinary

◆━━━━━━━━━━━━◆

God, thank You so much for Mary, this nobody of a girl from nowhere who became the mother of God. I thank You for her amazing example of humility and exuberant praise. She never drew attention to herself; instead, everything she said glorified You. She lived a poor, quiet life, but found favor in Your eyes and became a witness to the incarnation, the defining event of history. Only You, Lord, delight in turning our expectations on their head this way! Help me be more like Mary, Lord, and say continually, "Let it be to me according to Your word." Amen.

"For He who is mighty has done great things for me, and holy is His name."

Luke 1:49 NKJV

Lifting Weights of Sin

Dear Lord, I am struggling to forgive. I don't want to: I want to hold on to my resentment and continue to look at it and pet it and admire it. Help me, Lord. Each time I do this, Lord—allow You to come into a situation and help me forgive—it feels like the hardest thing I have ever done. I lay my burden at the cross, and suddenly I feel lighter. But then after a few minutes, or hours or days, I walk over and pick it up again. How could You do this for billions of people, when I can't even forgive *one* person and have it stick? I am looking to You, Jesus. Help me carry my cross daily in forgiveness and follow You. Amen.

"Forgive, and you will be forgiven."

LUKE 6:37 NIV

Instructions in Righteousness

On the same note, Lord, I want to thank You for this verse in Matthew. When You tell us to pray for our enemies (or even those we're just annoyed with), it works. I quite literally can't hold on to my negative feelings about a person when I'm lifting them up to You. Your Word is powerful and, when I obey it, I feel Your power at work in me. When I feel crushed by the weight of unforgiveness, like I don't have a hope or a prayer, this verse offers me both: it gives me a specific prayer to pray and tells what will happen if I do. I want to be Your child. Thank You for showing me how. Amen.

"But I tell you, love your enemies and pray for those who persecute you, that you may be children of your Father in heaven."

MATTHEW 5:44–45 NIV

Forgive

Forgive me, Lord, for harping on the same subject over and over. I am so slow to learn the lessons You are teaching. But You are patient and loving. . .and *long-suffering*. Thank You for not giving up on me as I learn to forgive others. I remember the first time You helped me win this battle. I remember being in the car, alone, and yelling, "I can't forgive him! I won't!" But You just kept insisting, quietly and firmly, *Forgive*. And then I did. I forgave and felt Your joy flood my heart. And I was *stronger*. Help me remember this victory, Lord, and keep strengthening my muscles for the harder battles to come. Amen.

You are from God, little children, and have overcome them; because greater is He who is in you than he who is in the world.

1 JOHN 4:4 NASB

A Bowl of Rice, Please

◆――――――――◆

Dear Father, there has never been a nation so blessed with *things* and opportunities and peace as this one. I don't know why You chose to let me live here, rather than, say, Angola or Eritrea or Afghanistan, but *thank* You. Yet, we are a nation with so many wants, and I am no different. Where someone in another country might want enough rice to fill her belly, a quiet night's sleep, or a doctor to treat an infected leg, we want *another* outfit to stuff in a jam-packed closet, the newest techno gadget, and a house with a pool. It will never be enough, Lord. Only You can fill the hole we try to fill with *stuff.* Thank You that I want for nothing except contentment. Amen.

But godliness with contentment is great gain.

1 Timothy 6:6 kjv

The Pebble

Sometimes I feel like I have no influence, Lord. That nothing I think or do resonates much beyond the walls of this house. But You comfort and empower me with Your Word, again. Thank You for reminding me that no matter what small circles we move in, we are all leaders to someone: a child, a wife, a younger brother, a boy flipping burgers in a fast-food joint, a shy new believer in church. I am a tiny pebble thrown into the sea, Lord, but my ripples will travel. Amen.

"You did not choose me, but I chose you and appointed you so that you might go and bear fruit—fruit that will last."

JOHN 15:16 NIV

Celebrating His
Glorious Work

Have you ever stopped to consider the cascade of miniscule reactions that takes place when you get a paper cut that prevents you from bleeding to death? Or the speed-of-light communications that allow you to snatch your hand away from a searing pan, unburned? Or the marvelous mechanism that enables two cells to join and grow in an interior pocket of flesh, then emerge as a separate creature with a unique soul? Or the perfection of balance that keeps the earth dancing around the sun instead of being pulled into a fiery embrace or flung into outer darkness? An old folk song calls God "the Lord of the dance." There is truth in that. As electrons spin around nuclei, planets around stars, and we spin in the circles of our comings and goings, God keeps it all in motion. Elegant. Elaborate. Ecstatic. Praise the Lord of the dance, and step into the circle of His arms.

The Missing Link

Dear Lord, sometimes I have to laugh at how hard people work to explain life apart from a Creator. They are desperate to throw in their lot with amoebas in a primordial soup pot rather than with a loving, creative God who might require something of them. But I thank You that You did create the universe out of nothing and us out of the dust of the earth. You spoke light into existence. Not in a billion years could we design a universe so complex, detailed, and interlocking. Thank You for the amazing love that keeps it all spinning. Amen.

Then God said, "Let there be light"; and there was light. God saw that the light was good; and God separated the light from the darkness.

GENESIS 1:3–4 NASB

Obsidian

Lord, my house is full of the flu, but I praise You with a kind of wide-eyed joy. I feel *patience* (where did *that* come from?) thickening like a skin over the lava of my usual anger, and I know that it can only come from You. I walk gingerly, Lord, because I don't yet trust myself. Will I fall through? Is it thick enough to hold? But thank You for what You are slowly forming beneath my feet: solid rock. Amen.

The Lord liveth; and blessed be my rock;
and exalted be the God of the rock of my salvation.

2 Samuel 22:47 kjv

Pack Nothing
but Faith

Dear Lord, Your world is so beautiful and *large*. Sometimes I sigh for all the places I will never see before I die. Mount Everest flying its white cloud-flag of spindrift. Greek islands floating in a wine-dark sea. A blue morpho flickering through the black-green-gold of the jungle. I miss them, somehow, though I've never seen them. But I know that nothing good will be lost, and I am confident that in heaven, I will ache for nothing left behind. I praise You for what *is* and for what will be. Amen.

Now faith is the assurance of things hoped for,
the conviction of things not seen.

HEBREWS 11:1 NASB

Flu Season

Now the flu's got me too, Lord, and I feel like I'm hanging on by the skin of my teeth, whatever that means. But You use everything to draw us closer to You, and even in this I can see You. Though I feel terrible right now, this virus will run its course; in a day or two I'll feel well again. But I won't *really* be well because I am also infected with another terrible disease, Lord, which will only be healed in glory: sin. I praise You, comforter, healer, sustainer, for what You are doing right now in my body and what You *will* do when I see You face-to-face. Amen.

The LORD will strengthen him on his bed of illness;
You will sustain him on his sickbed.

PSALM 41:3 NKJV

Unblemished

Lord, I praise You today for babies, for the gift of new life and the new life I have in You. I marvel at the perfect, round cheeks of my baby, his skin so smooth and firm and kissable. His silky hair lighter than air, his wide bright eyes. When he smiles, his face is all joy. Do You see me this way, Lord? Do I bring You this much joy? Sometimes I have a hard time believing that I—with my sags and bags and scars—am fearfully and wonderfully made. But I trust Your promises and Your love. I trust the blood of Jesus that has washed me into new life. Amen.

And He who sits on the throne said,
"Behold, I am making all things new."

Revelation 21:5 nasb

What Will Be

Dear Father, the more I know about Your creation, the more I marvel at the mind that conceived it. The more I marvel at You. Your creation is irreducibly complex, multifaceted, and breathtakingly beautiful whether viewed from a satellite or in a microscope. And we are only just beginning *to begin* to fathom its mysteries. I praise You for the spirit of inquiry that You fashioned in us along with the breath of life. I praise You that You are *knowable.* And I praise You for the day when we will know You fully. Amen.

> *The earth will be full of the knowledge*
> *of the Lord as the waters cover the sea.*
>
> Isaiah 11:9 nasb

I Will Lift Up Mine Eyes

Lord, I praise You for mountains. I praise You for the old, rolling backs of the Appalachians. I praise You for the sharp, unworn spires of the Himalayas. I praise You for snow-capped peaks and glacier-grooved summits and the way mountains train my eyes *upward*. Lord, I so often fix my eyes on the pebbles at my feet, on the trivialities that trip me and dog my path. Give me Your eyes, Lord. Give me the long view. Thank You for this trail I am on, Lord, the sights along the way, and the vista that awaits at the end. Amen.

Let the rivers clap their hands,
let the mountains sing together for joy.

PSALM 98:8 NIV

Overtaken

So often, Lord, when I imagine witnessing to someone, I think I have to have every argument and counterargument planned out twelve moves in advance, like it's a chess game. I think of potential questions, and if I don't have perfect answers for them, that's enough to keep me from opening my mouth at all. But Your Word is so clear: *we* do not convert the lost. The Gospel is *alive*. It converts. It overtakes. Lord, I trust Your Word and its mighty power to do what I cannot. Amen.

*But My words and My statutes, which I commanded
My servants the prophets, did they not overtake
and take hold of your fathers? So they repented.*

ZECHARIAH 1:6 AMPC

A Joyful Noise

Dear God, I thank You for music. For the music of rain on rooftops and wind in bare branches. For the splash of water over stones. For little children shouting a hymn at the top of their lungs. For a Bach organ concerto. Lord, Your creation praises You all the time, with every breath and in every moment. Thank You for letting me join in this eternal song of praise. Hallelujah! Worthy is the Lamb who was slain!

Shout joyfully to the Lord,
all the earth; break forth in song,
rejoice, and sing praises.

PSALM 98:4 NKJV

Dry Mouth

◆————————◆

Lord, You can use anyone to spread the good news. You can use invalids, the elderly, fishermen, the mentally challenged, paupers, rich men, tax collectors, children, even me. Thank You that You don't require me to know everything or have every answer. You don't require me to be well traveled or well dressed. You don't require a seminary degree. You don't require me to be anything but saved by the blood of Jesus. The only requirement for evangelism is that I believe, and speak. Lord, I believe. Now open my mouth. Amen.

We also believe and therefore speak.

2 Corinthians 4:13 nkjv

Giraffes and Hedgehogs

Dear Lord, I praise You for laughter. Tonight I laughed until my sides ached, and it was *good*. Now I feel cleansed and emptied of distress and strangely content. Thank You for being a God whose miracles bring laughter: Sarah with the news of her improbable baby, Lazarus raised to life, and the disciples with their ridiculous catch of fish. I can imagine You standing there, Lord, and laughing until the tears came with the people You love. Thank You for giraffes and hedgehogs and zebras and penguins, and how You long to astonish us with joy. Amen.

Then our mouth was filled with laughter
and our tongue with joyful shouting.

PSALM 126:2 NASB

Well Begun Is Half Done

Dear God, there is something You've asked me to do that I've been putting off for a long time. You haven't forgotten—though *I've* certainly tried to. You keep gently reminding and prodding me to obey. Tonight, as I was walking and pondering this in the darkness between streetlights, I was filled with a cheerful certainty that by the next day, I would have begun. And this wasn't wishful thinking, was it, Lord? It was *faith*. Thank You for believing in what is not yet visible in me and allowing me to do the same. Amen.

Now faith is the substance of things hoped for,
the evidence of things not seen.

HEBREWS 11:1 NKJV

The Giver

Lord, I've never been hungry (unless I was dieting); I've never been naked (except by choice); I've never been without shelter (excluding backpacking trips). You have been a faithful provider of the things You know I need. Thank You for my parents, who provided for me from birth to age twenty-three. And thank You for my husband, who has so faithfully provided for me in the years since then. Thank You, Lord, for providing for me through their generosity and hard work. It's humbling to realize that I've never been completely self-sufficient at any point in my life, yet there is a lesson in that too. We are paupers by nature: *all* is from You. I praise my openhanded God! Amen.

You open your hand and satisfy the
desires of every living thing.

PSALM 145:16 NIV

Celebration

Dear Father, so many people who don't know You see You as a heavenly killjoy: stopping them from doing really fun things that would bring them great enjoyment. But we know You better! Thank You that You do not delight in denial: You delight in saying yes to Your people. But more importantly, You delight in *us* and what is for our ultimate good, not just fun for a moment. And You are planning the ultimate party—one that will last forever. I can't wait to join the celebration! Amen.

They celebrate your abundant goodness
and joyfully sing of your righteousness.

PSALM 145:7 NIV

His Work

God, I am amazed that You never tire of listening to me. *I* get tired of listening to me, Lord! The same fears, the same complaints, the same problems, the same confusions—year after year. Yet, even I see progress, and I praise You. I am not who I was, and I know it's all because of You. Thank You for how You continue to work in me: so faithfully, patiently, lovingly. You are the potter; I am the grateful clay in Your hands. Amen.

"For the eyes of the Lord are on the righteous
and his ears are attentive to their prayer."

1 Peter 3:12 niv

Praise for Yesterday,
Today, and Tomorrow

The boy was disgusted by the smell of pigs by the end of the first day. By the end of the second, he hated them. By the third, he envied their full stomachs. By the fourth, he was sneaking bits of their food when his master's back was turned. By the end of the fifth day, he was crying for rescue. Then the Bible says he "came to himself," remembering who he was and where he had come from: the beloved son of a rich and generous father. And he didn't die, but returned and lived. He could bear the day because he knew where he'd come from and whom he belonged to. His past gave him hope for the future. In God's economy, nothing is wasted: not the pods that the pigs eat, not the stench, not the knees worn rough with praying. It is all good if it brings us to Him.

On the Loom

Lord, I thank You for my yesterdays, todays, and tomorrows. Sometimes I look at the shape of my life, and I see a mess: colors appear then disappear, patterns peter out, threads end in impenetrable tangles. But I know You see it differently. You see the tapestry that faces the light, while I just see the chaos of warp and weft that hides in the dark against the wall. I praise You for the glimpses You give me of how You are weaving it all together. And I long for the day when I will see Your handiwork unveiled. Thank You for being the master weaver of my life. Amen.

To the end that my glory may sing
praise to thee, and not be silent.
O LORD my God, I will give
thanks unto thee for ever.

PSALM 30:12 KJV

The Grand Timeline

Lord, thank You for the grand story of history, which is really *Your* story. I see exploration, discovery, and war all muddled together, repeating, and leading *where?* But You had the end in mind from the beginning. I know I can trust that You are leading us to an end, and to a good place. And I praise You for the amazing grace that has allowed my story to be a small part of the story You are telling. Amen.

He has made everything beautiful in its time. He has also set eternity in the human heart; yet no one can fathom what God has done from beginning to end.

ECCLESIASTES 3:11 NIV

The Living Fossil

———◆———

Lord, You have preserved Your Word for thousands of years. It is uncorrupted; it is unchanged; it has not been forgotten. Like an animal buried and hammered into rock by time and pressure, it has come down to us, yet it is not fossilized: it lives! You chiseled Your law into rock for Moses, but now Your Word is written in our hearts. And we too will live uncorrupted and unforgotten but, thanks be to You, *changed*. Amen.

You are an epistle of Christ. . .written not with ink but by the Spirit of the living God, not on tablets of stone but on tablets of flesh, that is, of the heart.

2 CORINTHIANS 3:3 NKJV

At the Intersection of Faith and Chutzpah

———◆———◆———

Dear Father, I see Your chosen people living in their little land, surrounded by so many enemies, and it seems like a situation ripe for disaster. Except I know Your Word, and I know how You love them! I praise You for how You have protected Israel for thousands of years. I praise You for fire from heaven, dry ground in the midst of the sea, and for the miracles You will do for Your people in these latter days. Thank You for allowing me to be alive *now.* Next year in the New Jerusalem!

> *"Who among the gods is like you, LORD?*
> *Who is like you—majestic in holiness,*
> *awesome in glory, working wonders?"*

EXODUS 15:11 NIV

Luther, Wesley, Crosby, Etc.

Dear God, I don't know where I'd be tonight without the great hymns of the faith that have resounded in my head since I was a girl. Thank You for that legacy of music and poetry and for what You have taught me through meditating on those lines. I praise You for the men and women who penned the lyrics and music that still minister to Christians today. Thank You for the hymns that kept my heart tuned to You, even when I thought I was running far away. Great is Thy faithfulness! Amen.

Let the word of Christ dwell in you richly in all wisdom;
teaching and admonishing one another in psalms
and hymns and spiritual songs, singing with
grace in your hearts to the Lord.

COLOSSIANS 3:16 KJV

Getting to Know You

Dear Lord, thank You for reminding me today to pray for the people who witnessed to me before I was a believer. I was so ignorant of Your ways, Lord, that I didn't even know that was what they were doing! I thought they were just telling me about their lives, that we were getting to know each other, when really they were introducing me to their Savior. I praise You for how real You were to them and for their example of how sharing our faith is more about *conversation* than conversion. Bless those brave evangelists, Lord, and continue to do Your work through them. Amen.

Because we loved you so much, we were delighted to share with you not only the gospel of God but our lives as well.

1 THESSALONIANS 2:8 NIV

Here Are My Mother and Brothers

✦————————✦

Dear Father, sometimes I feel like I'd do better on a desert island. It's hard to live in community. Our rough edges meet the rough edges of others, and the results are scrapes and sparks and *wounds*. Thank You so much for the pictures You present in the Gospels of Jesus living with His disciples. Lord, nothing teaches me more about what pleases You and what is *possible* than studying how You did it, how You lived and loved and ate and traveled, together. Help me think of the people I rub elbows with as *my* disciples, companions, and teachers. Amen.

Pointing to his disciples, he said, "Here are my mother and my brothers. For whoever does the will of my Father in heaven is my brother and sister and mother."

MATTHEW 12:49–50 NIV

Little Altars All Over

———◆———

Lord, how easily we forget Your faithfulness. I think *I* would never be like the Israelites, longing for the slave-grown melons and cucumbers of Egypt while following the fire of God through the desert. But my memory is just as short, just as fickle. You knew they needed reminders, so their path was littered with altars and memorials, their calendar marked with feasts and holidays and fasts. *"Don't forget who I Am and what I have done,"* You say. Lord, please show me tangible ways to remember Your faithfulness to me too. Amen.

Then let us arise and go up to Bethel, and I will make there an altar to God Who answered me in the day of my distress and was with me wherever I went.

Genesis 35:3 ampc

With This Ring

❖

Dear Lord, You are faithful yesterday, today, and tomorrow. I thank You for giving me a husband who exemplifies that enduring faithfulness. Thank You for how he has kept the promises he made to me on our wedding day: promises to love, cherish, protect, and provide. Thank You for his hands that hold my heart so gently; thank You that he is more like Jesus than anyone I have ever known. I praise You for the great gift that he is to me. Thank You for his example of faithful love, and I pray that I would give him only joy, submission, and devotion in return. Amen.

For no matter how many promises God
has made, they are "Yes" in Christ.

2 CORINTHIANS 1:20 NIV

Twenty-Four

I thank You for this day, Lord, with its twenty-four precious, exhausting hours. Only twenty-four. That never seems like enough, yet I'm always glad to fall into bed when they're over. Some hours spent in sleep, some in work, some in eating, some in talking, some in staring out the kitchen window at the trees and sky. How many of those hours do I give to You, Lord? *One*, maybe two, on Sundays? Thank You for continuing to remind me that relationships require *time*, and I vow to give You more of each day—each day that is already a gift from You. Amen.

This is the day which the LORD hath made;
we will rejoice and be glad in it.

PSALM 118:24 KJV

The Time of Singing

◆————————————————◆

Father, the earth is brown and dead now, as hard as iron and as cold as stone. But I know that life lurks, waits: seeds that will spring to green life with the warming sun and a gentle rain, nests that will hold eggs the color of sky, ponds that will sparkle and sing with dragonflies and frogs. Thank You for spring, for the promise of green and new life. And thank You for heaven, where that fleeting green will never fade and fall away. Amen.

"For lo, the winter is past, the rain is over and gone. The flowers appear on the earth; the time of singing has come."

SONG OF SOLOMON 2:11–12 NKJV

The Day of
Small Things

Dear Lord, I ask for thankfulness in the small things. I yearn to see each day as a gift—swathed in sunrise—to be unwrapped. Thank You, Lord, for what You gave me today: for a curl of green leaf unfurling on the winter-end of a branch, for a cherry blossom like a snag of fuchsia silk, for scratchy frog songs. Thank You for moments that remind me that ordinary days are really shot through with holiness. I thank You now, Lord, for those gifts and the gifts that I will see *You've already given me* as I learn to live in thankfulness. Amen.

*For who hath despised the day of small
things? for they shall rejoice.*

ZECHARIAH 4:10 KJV

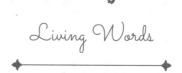

Living Words

Dear God, Your Word is thousands of years old and tells stories even older. How many books made millennia ago are still useful today? Curious, maybe, or *interesting,* but still practical? Lord, I can't think of even one. We read old poems, histories, and sagas for school assignments or because we want to learn about the past or because they tell good stories, but how many lives have been changed from reading *Beowulf* or *The Canterbury Tales*? Your Word is as true today as when the ink was wet. It is beautiful. It is inspiring. It is rich. It surprises. It sustains. It transforms. I praise the living Word.

*O LORD, You are my God. I will exalt You, I will praise
Your name, for You have done wonderful things;
Your counsels of old are faithfulness and truth.*

ISAIAH 25:1 NKJV

The Dead Will Live!

Dear Lord, I was feeling so sad this morning. Maybe it was partly the rain and the gray skies, but I was missing certain people so badly. My dad, my grandmothers, my great-aunts, friends. They are all dead, Lord, and that seems so strange and wrong. They are in the ground, out of sight, out of reach. Thank You for comforting me with the assurance that it *is* wrong, that death was not part of Your plan. And that, ultimately, it will be swallowed up in victory. My dad, my grandmothers, they will wake up and shout for joy. Hallelujah!

*But your dead will live, L*ORD*; their bodies will rise—*
let those who dwell in the dust wake up and shout for joy.

ISAIAH 26:19 NIV

The Wedding March

Dear Father, my kids are all still little and know nothing of romantic desire. They are still in love with me and their father. But I know the day is coming, Lord, when they will transfer their affections to someone else, and I lift those yet-unknown *someones* up to You. Bless their future spouses with faith and wisdom and purity as they wait. I pray that You would help me show my children what marriage can be, and that You would hold their hearts, Lord, until You join them with another. Amen.

He who finds a wife finds a good thing,
and obtains favor from the LORD.

PROVERBS 18:22 NKJV

Amen

The man prayed until the room grew cold and his feet
went numb. He prayed beyond darkness into the pale
purple of the next day. He prayed until it was time
to return to the hospital and greet a new round
of doctors trying to save his wife's life.
As always, the last word he said before he struggled
to his feet was "Amen." Had he ever ended any prayer
differently? What was amen, really? A closing, like
sincerely or yours truly? A spiritual-sounding goodbye?
A way to end a conversation? He looked out at the dawn.
Amen was all that: love, goodbye, thank you. It was a
statement of God's faithfulness and his own affirmation
of that faithfulness. In it he saw a releasing of the hands,
a letting go. The prayer was a butterfly, held gently,
then uncupped to fly upward. And amen was a
word, almost just a sound, to guide his
thoughts into the heart of God.

The Confidence of Firsthand Knowledge

◆

Lord, it all comes down to knowing You. Who I am, where I'm headed, and what You require of me all depend on who You are. I don't ask for supernatural revelation, Lord (though I wouldn't turn it down). I just ask for a dogged determination to know You better, verse by verse. I ask—beg, really—for a continual filling of Your Spirit so that my eyes and heart are wide open to You. Then I can say *amen* with confidence. And I will: Amen!

I've got my eye on the goal, where God is beckoning us
onward—to Jesus. I'm off and running,
and I'm not turning back.

PHILIPPIANS 3:14 MSG

Listen to the Music

Dear Father, I'm lifting up a teenager to You tonight who gives You lip service but whose heart doesn't belong to You yet. She knows what to say when Christians are watching, but I know her answers are different when she is in other company. Lord, You are watching her. Remind her of this. Hound her, Lord, until she turns her heart to You. But in this I praise You: she only listens to Christian music. Her soul is yearning for You, whether she knows it or not. Fan that small spark of desire into an eternal *yes*. Amen.

The Spirit and the bride say, "Come." And let the one who hears say, "Come." And let the one who is thirsty come; let the one who wishes take the water of life without cost.

REVELATION 22:17 NASB

Worry Lines

Dear Lord, I praise You for how You are changing me. I praise You for how You are teaching me to place a worry in my open hand and lift it up to You: if it stays or if it flies away, it belongs to You. I trust You with my life. Lord, the only worry lines I want are the creases in the pages of my Bible. I praise You that *You* are the overcomer; *You* are my resting place; *You* are my strength and my fortress. I am so relieved to lay my worries before You and let them become prayers. Amen.

Don't fret or worry. Instead of worrying, pray.
Let petitions and praises shape your worries into
prayers, letting God know your concerns.

PHILIPPIANS 4:6 MSG

Foot Washing

Dear Father, when everything is going well, and people are behaving the way I think they should, I find it easy to love. But when the seas are rougher and the sailors are seasick or muttering mutiny, I am appalled at how quickly I become apathetic or mean-spirited. Forgive me, Lord. I want to love like You do. You washed *Judas's* feet! You gently washed the grimy toes of the man who sold You for thirty pieces of silver. What kind of love is that? I could never do that. But Your Spirit, working through my hands, *could*. I praise You for that and so much more.

"By this everyone will know that you are my disciples, if you love one another."

JOHN 13:35 NIV

Baby Blue

Lord, I lift up to You a new mother who is struggling with postpartum depression. With a thirty-six-hour labor, she went from a full-throttle life to a torn body, alien responsibilities, and sleep deprivation. Help her hold on while she heals and adjusts. Surround her with people who will love and support her in practical ways. Be with her husband as he copes with a new baby and a wife who needs him now in ways he never imagined. Bless that little one with health and sleep. Lord, use this time, so that they will look back on it and marvel at how You drew them closer to each other and to You. Amen.

He tends his flock like a shepherd: He gathers the lambs in his arms and carries them close to his heart; he gently leads those that have young.

ISAIAH 40:11 NIV

Don't Touch My Feet

Lord, I'm still thinking about foot washing. I can imagine washing someone else's feet, but the idea of having someone—especially You—wash *my* feet makes me squirm. That is appalling grace, like Your offering Yourself up on the cross for us, an act of love so unbelievable that I sometimes don't know what to do with it. How can I say thank you adequately for that? I don't think I ever can. But I will keep trying: thank You, thank You, thank You. Please take away the embarrassment and pride that so often keep me from running to You for the cleansing I desperately need. Amen.

*Jesus answered, "Unless I wash you,
you have no part with me."*

JOHN 13:8 NIV

How's the Service?

◆————————◆

Dear Lord, I do a lot of things for a lot of people every day. I serve, then serve some more. But, Lord, I am asking You right now to show me my heart. Is my service pleasing to You? Am I serving under obligation, as one who is a slave to sin? Or am I serving with the voluntary spirit of my freedom in Christ? I long to serve without counting the cost. But it's so easy to pray this sort of prayer, Lord, and then go and *do nothing*. Please show me who and how to serve, then help me do it in Jesus' name. Amen.

"For the Lord searches all hearts and understands all the intent of the thoughts. If you seek Him, He will be found by you."

1 Chronicles 28:9 nkjv

The Hollow

Jesus, when I think about You making Your home in my heart, I imagine a little creature padding a tree hollow with leaves and dry grasses and turning in a tight, furry circle and falling asleep. The tree is strong—an oak, perhaps, or a towering hemlock—and will stand, unbowed through the winter storms. I am that furry creature, Lord: a well-beloved, dear thing. And You are the tree. It is not so much that You live in *me*, but that I live in *You*. Thank You for letting me burrow into Your deep, safe, warm heart, Lord, and remain. Amen.

Keep me as the apple of your eye;
hide me in the shadow of your wings.

PSALM 17:8 NIV

A Collective Amen

Dear Lord, in Your infinite wisdom, You let me be born in New England. I know I breathed in a portion of northeastern stubborn independence along with frigid air and the odd blackfly. You know how I struggle with working as part of a group. I want to do things my way, by myself. But I was struck, Lord, with how many verses in Your Word end with something like, "And let all the people say *Amen!*" You are trying to reveal a truth about the power that believers wield when we gather together in prayer. Alone, we are strong, but together we are mightier than an army with banners. Help me join in with joy. Praise the Lord!

Blessed be the LORD, the God of Israel,
from everlasting even to everlasting. And let
all the people say, "Amen." Praise the LORD!

PSALM 106:48 NASB

The Amen Incarnate

Dear Father, so many portraits paint Jesus as a soft, almost wilting, white man. But I bet You weren't: I bet You were dark and as hard as nails. I bet Your feet were cut and Your hands were scarred, even before the cross. Yet You are also the image of the invisible God. You are the Amen, the *so be it*. There is an equation here, the solution of which is just beyond my grasp. Jesus equals the image of God equals Amen equals *so be it*. I am so glad You are not easy to figure out. I am so thankful that You offer mystery and puzzles and food for thought that will satisfy my soul for eternity. Amen.

*"These are the words of the Amen,
the faithful and true witness,
the ruler of God's creation."*

REVELATION 3:14 NIV

So Be It

Dearest Lord, I know what I want, but I can't see the future. I know what I think would be best for me and the people around me, but I don't have Your eyes. So I pray, but I hold my prayers lightly. Are they Your will? Am I praying rightly? Show me, Lord. When I pray *Amen*, I think what I really mean is *Your will be done*. And it's a conundrum: I know Your will *will* be done, yet You ask me to pray also. Why, Lord? I long to obey with knowledge, but for now I will simply obey. And wait on You. Amen.

The effective, fervent prayer of a
righteous man avails much.

JAMES 5:16 NKJV

Detours on the Way to Amen

Father, I never seem to be able to get to *Amen* in one go. With people around me all day long (and no prayer closets with locks), quiet times are more like dull-roar times. But when I study Your Word, Lord, I am often so surprised: Jesus going off alone into the wilderness to pray, then being followed by the disciples who, like little children, can't seem to get enough of Him. They interrupt His prayers with questions and comments, and He never once says, "Go away; can't you see I'm praying?" So thank You for the interruptions, Lord; I'm welcoming them as a chance to be like Jesus. Interrupt me, Lord, and conform my character into that of Your precious Son. Amen.

Strengthened with all might, according to his glorious power, unto all patience and longsuffering with joyfulness.

COLOSSIANS 1:11 KJV

Faster, Donkey?

◆

Jesus, did You ever hurry? Were You ever in a rush as You walked from Cana to Capernaum? Were You ever late for dinner with Mary and Martha? Did You ever kick Your heels into the donkey's side so it would trot just a bit faster? I don't think so, Lord. Your Word shows You differently: wherever You were was exactly where You wanted to be at that moment, even on the cross. I long to be like that. Please help me slow down and savor this life You have blessed me with: the small moments of glory, quiet words with a friend, even the daily struggles that are conforming me to Your image. I am *here*, and so are You. Amen.

"Be still, and know that I am God."

Psalm 46:10 niv

After the Amen

So, Father, where do I go from here? How do I live once I get up off my knees? I like quick fixes, amazing tricks that promise to solve problems in three easy steps. But I know You are not like that. Sometimes, the miraculous intervenes, but more often the Christian life is—as I heard one author put it—a long obedience in the same direction. Maybe what You've shown me most clearly, Lord, is not to wait for everything to be "perfect" before I try to follow You more faithfully. Help me to—standing, sitting, lying down, or running—*live* as though I'm on my knees. Amen.

"Who among all these does not know that the hand of the LORD has done this, in whose hand is the life of every living thing, and the breath of all mankind?"

JOB 12:9–10 NASB

Falling into Light

❖━━━━━━━━━━❖

Dear Lord, again I thank You for Your precious Word. Thank You for the prayer You gave us in Ephesians 3 and how it has enriched my understanding of You. When I fall to my knees, You will strengthen me. That is such a glorious picture of the fruits of both worship and humility. I fall, Lord, because I am weak and because You are great, and then in falling, miraculously, Your strength becomes mine. You dwell in me. Your boundless love bears fruit in me: enough both to keep and to give away. I—weak, broken, sin-scarred, blind— am strong, whole, pure, clear-eyed, and filled with the fullness of God. Praise God!

Therefore He says: "Awake, you who sleep, arise from the dead, and Christ will give you light."

EPHESIANS 5:14 NKJV

A Long Way Off

Dear Lord, I can't even remember where I was two months ago when I began this journey to draw closer to You. I was in a different place; *I* was different. Just like the prodigal son, I am still a long way off. I am far from where You want me and far, even, from where I want to be—and I'm usually pretty easy on myself. But I praise You for drawing me closer. I praise You for how Your Word has soothed the rough, bitter edges of my heart and washed away years of silt and sin. Please help me go forward from here, drinking deeper and believing harder that He who promises is faithful. Amen.

"When he was still a great way off, his father saw him and had compassion, and ran and fell on his neck and kissed him."

LUKE 15:20 NKJV

The End of the Matter

---

*For this reason I kneel before the Father, from whom
every family in heaven and on earth derives its name.
I pray that out of his glorious riches he may strengthen
you with power through his Spirit in your inner being,
so that Christ may dwell in your hearts through faith.
And I pray that you, being rooted and established in
love, may have power, together with all the Lord's holy
people, to grasp how wide and long and high and deep
is the love of Christ, and to know this love that surpasses
knowledge—that you may be filled to the measure of
all the fullness of God. Now to him who is able to do
immeasurably more than all we ask or imagine,
according to his power that is at work within us,
to him be glory in the church and in Christ Jesus
throughout all generations, for ever and ever! Amen.*

EPHESIANS 3:14–21 NIV

About the Author

Laura Freudig lives on an island off the coast of Maine with her husband and five children. She graduated from Amherst College and has lived in Maryland, Massachusetts, New York, Virginia, Washington, and England. She loves hiking, homeschooling, reading, multitasking, gardening, good coffee, and singing.